CHURCH
VS.
STATE

FAITH AND FREEDOM
SERIES

CHURCH VS. STATE

JOHN W. WHITEHEAD

MOODY PRESS
CHICAGO

For legal assistance or educational materials,
contact The Rutherford Institute at:

P.O. Box 7482
Charlottesville, Virginia 22906-7482
(804) 978-3888

* * * * * * *

© 1996 by
JOHN W. WHITEHEAD

ISBN: 0-8024-6689-3

1 3 5 7 9 10 8 6 4 2

Printed in the United States of America

It is told that, when the American troops began to run out of wadding paper for their muskets during a skirmish with the British in Springfield, New Jersey, during the American Revolution, chaplain James Caldwell gathered up hymnals written by Isacc Watts and gave them to the soldiers, crying, "Now put Watts into them, boys!"[1] Even though the pulpits of America were often the rallying points for the cause of the American Revolution, the "peace" churches, such as the Mennonites and Quakers, as well as other Christian ministers and laypersons, ministered to soldiers in need on both sides of the Revolution—often at the risk of being convicted of treason or of being killed or wounded.[2] Paul Revere used the steeple of Boston's Old North Church to inform the Charlestown Sons of Liberty as to the path the Redcoats would take to attack Boston.[3] The effect of churches upon resistance and the American Revolution is part of our American history. For example:

> The New England clergy's opposition to British measures is well documented. The quiet efforts of Dr. Samuel Cooper of Brattle Street Church and the more public patriotism of Charles Chauncy added significantly to resistance activ-

ity in Boston. The Reverend Johnas Clark of Lexington was the Revolutionary scribe of his town, writing up petitions and instructions on political subjects throughout the era and making his house a center for political gatherings. Two fiery young Congregational ministers converted entire towns in western Massachusetts from tory to whig by haranguing the people in town meeting and Sabbath convocation alike. . . . Along the frontier preachers played an especially critical role as missionaries for the Revolution, carrying the whig gospel to hamlets and homesteads beyond the reach of newspapers and committees of correspondence. . . . Thus did the colonial clergy during the Revolutionary years perform functions of a sort they had already been exercising for some time. It was still the case some fifty years later, according to Alexis de Tocqueville, that in the American West you would "meet a politician where you expected to find a priest."[4]

Today, there are an estimated 50 million evangelicals in the United States.[5] Another category of Americans, homosexuals, is estimated to include only some 2 percent to 10 percent of the total American population, which would make their number somewhere between 4.5 million to 22 million. A comparison between the relative political, social and artistic influence of these groups reveals an astonishing disparity. In contrast to the rich influence of America's historical churches, contemporary American culture reveals a greatly diminished church influence.

In contemporary America, the mission of many churches manifests too few differences from secular social programs. Much of organized "religion" is now focused primarily on social needs:

> Some successful boomer churches are shrines to secular movements, particularly the 12-step program modeled on Alcoholics Anonymous. "We refer to ourselves as wounded healers," says Minister Mike Matoin of Unity in Chicago, himself a former bellhop, bouncer, cabdriver, and child of an alcoholic. "A lot of baby boomers can relate to us. We've been through our own recovery, and we're not on a pedestal." If a spiritual search is going on, it is for an inner child.[6]

The concept that the Bible is true and that God's demands revealed therein must be obeyed has become so muffled that many "religious" persons today really identify only with the American civil religion—nothing more than an acknowledgment of God on ceremonial occasions and at times of personal or national crisis. Thus, Mark Twain's comment on the motto that appears on America's money seems even more apt today: "It is simple, direct, gracefully phrased. It always sounds well—In God We Trust. I don't believe it would sound any better if it were true."[7]

There are, of course, many reasons for this. First, there is the matter of contemporary religious belief itself. As noted above, significant religious belief in modern times has given way to a cultural religion for many people. In questioning Americans about the importance of religion in their individual lives, pollster George Gallup found that:

> [A]s a people, we lack deep levels of individual spiritual commitment. One sign of this is that the level of ethics in this country seems to be declining—at least in terms of public perceptions of ethical behavior. . . . [W]e found there's very little difference between the churched and the unchurched in terms of their general views on ethical matters, and also their practical ethical responses in various situations.[8]

Second, seminaries, pastors, and church leaders often do little to teach and nurture true spiritualism. Too many pastors dispense ersatz psychology instead of teaching the commands of Judeo-Christian theology. Too many "Christian" seminaries have trained their students to do so. Many church members and their leaders are too illiterate in their faith to combat the uncompromising demands of secularism.

Third, Phariseeism remains a problem for many Christians and their churches. Although the Old Testament Pharisees were a visible and important part of their social structure, they nonetheless created and flourished in

8

self-righteous enclaves of their own making. Their lives centered around what amounted to a holy club. They were harsh and censorious to those outside the club. Too many contemporary evangelicals do the same. They create their own set of rules that are either extrabiblical or rely on particular Bible verses that have conveniently been removed from their contexts. These external checkpoints are used to indicate a supposed spirituality, but they often create nothing more than the facade of holiness, just as they did for the Pharisees of old. This legalism makes it easy to judge others and easy to retreat into modern-day holy clubs. And the club atmosphere is not only used to separate the holy from the nonholy. It also often separates Christians themselves along racial, ethnic, and economic lines.

Fourth, too many Christians and their churches have withdrawn from the world. Outsiders easily sense when a church is a refuge *from* them rather than a ministry *for* them:

> To the outsider the church is often not inviting but forbidding, smugly satisfied with itself and harshly condemning of others. Non-Christians sometimes say that they find more acceptable, more compassionate understanding of human foibles in the world than in the church. To them the church is lacking in warmth, even positively inhuman.[9]

Fifth, sectarianism has produced believers who attack each other over arcane theological interpretations instead of doing battle with the enemy. The factionalization of modern-day Christianity could not be attractive to those who do not yet believe and should not be attractive to those who do.

Sixth, many churches have interpreted modern catastrophes and political events as signaling the end times, which has, in turn, led not only to withdrawal, but also to disinterest in the concerns of the modern world. Jesus Christ said only the Father knew the day and the hour of the end.[10] Nonetheless, many augment their withdrawal from the world by arming themselves in preparation for the Armageddon or by simply refusing to participate in the betterment of society or evangelizing.

Seventh, at the other extreme, too many Christians busy themselves with activities designed to take over and rule the world, or at least America. They want to take "dominion" over the political process until the "righteous," namely themselves, hold the reigns of power and reinstitute Old Testament law. God could then rule through them, his chosen intermediaries. Utopianism, reconstructionism, or whatever other name the notion uses, is incorrect biblically. The Bible is clear that no person possesses righteousness

10

and that true Christians are only re-
pentant sinners. The dominion im-
pulse to subdue the earth, spoken of in
the first chapter of Genesis, has been
tainted by the Fall. It has produced
campaigns of terror when not re-
strained by a concept of Christian justice. Moreover, the historical record
proves that power can corrupt even the
most virtuous. The believer's claim
must not be for political domination,
but for equal access to the world's marketplace of ideas, where true Christianity, and the worldview that springs
from it, can more than hold its own.

Eighth, too many churches have
succumbed to the lure of show business. While "religious" television and
radio talk shows and televangelism
programs proliferate, fewer and fewer
apparently appreciate the desecrating
and debilitating effect being wreaked
upon the majesty and mystery of the
Judeo-Christian religion. As Professor
Neil Postman, author of *Amusing Ourselves to Death*, notes, television strips
away everything that makes religion a
historic, profound, and sacred activity.
On television, "there is no ritual, no dog-
ma, no tradition, no theology, and above
all, no sense of spiritual transcen-
dence."[11] Instead of changing the medium for the better, tele-Christianity has
adapted itself to the medium and become entertainment with the talk-show
format, the glitzy and too often ridic-
ulous "stars" hosting the celebrity

guests. These, not God, are the stars of the show. The show business requirements for audience-share also necessitate giving the audience what it wants, rather than what the Gospel demands. This, too often, is the "name it and claim it" gospel of wealth. Far too many churches, on the local and national level, are built around a celebrity pastor or music director.

Ninth, too many churches promote "heart" knowledge over "head" knowledge, thus promoting the highly anti-in-tellectual, sentimental and secularized view that certain disciplines and areas of inquiry are off-limits to Christians. As Professor Postman notes:

> In the eighteenth and nineteenth centuries, religious thought and institutions in America were dominated by an austere, learned, and intellectual form of discourse that is largely absent from religious life today.[12]

Many modern pastors "dumb down" their sermons rather than challenge their congregations with rigorous intellectual fare; they aim their sermons at everyone in general, so that they aim at no one in particular. God's revelation of Himself in human form and in human history is a stupendous event that is available to the intellect of every human being, and each human being should use all of his or her intellect to understand it.

Tenth, too many churches are culturally illiterate. Modern culture has simply by-passed theology. Traditional and historical Judeo-Christian beliefs hold that the arts, human creativity, and the beauty of the creation are gifts of God and thus need no justification on spiritual or utilitarian grounds. They are valuable in themselves and were put here for people's enjoyment and perhaps enlightenment. But much of modern artistic accomplishment belongs to nonbelievers. Too often in modern Christianity there is a lack of craftsmanship and serious artistic merit. Examples of Christian artistic and literary work found in many Christian bookstores and gift shops is too often simply "Jesus junk." Even when the world's artistic standards are low, it does not mean that Christians should accept mediocrity and then spiritualize it. The work of the Reformers, for example, in holding up the noble and redemptive purposes of artistic endeavors of all kinds should be the model for modern-day Christians—even those who have little artistic talent. Many Christians have no view of the arts because they do not view the arts. They do not go to movies or ballet or theater. They do not listen to music other than so-called Christian music. Churches must understand the culture around them, a task that could be accomplished to a large degree by understanding—

not necessarily adopting or accepting —the artistic work of the day.

Finally, many modern churches have accepted the view that bigger and "slicker" is better: national movements are better than local church activities; mass media is more effective than local media; and television-church is better than a church with no television program. The Bible is clear that it is the responsibility of the local church to train, equip, and support its members. The Bible is clear that relationships are local; it is the Christian *duty* that knows no boundaries or locales.

The world today is obviously under God's judgment. Few, if any, knowledgeable Christians would disagree with this assessment. But this is not cause for comfort. The Bible is clear that God's judgment begins not with the world and those who oppose God, but rather with "us," the family of God, the local church."

Given the terrible condition of the world, the inadequate efforts of the church, and the sure hand of God's judgment, it seems that the only authentic response is a return to true Christianity.

The United States was, at one time in its history, a nation greatly influenced by Christianity. This stemmed from those who immigrated from Europe and established the original colonial governments. Up through the nineteenth century, the Judeo-Chris-

14

tian belief system and ethic pervaded the American culture.

At one time, the Christian church, with leadership from pastors, helped provide a form of stability for the culture. Times have changed. For the reasons mentioned above, the Christian church, its leaders, and its members too often fail to provide an effective model or the necessary leadership for this nation. Churches, along with religious persons individually, are either retreating from public view or are being separated through the force of law from the mainstream of American culture.

At the same time, secularists and those who believe that religion is strictly a private matter are more than willing to facilitate and implement the retreat of Christians and the Christian church. Laws and governmental policies abound that muzzle, or at least muffle, the message and work of the church. Much of this masquerades under the so-called doctrine of the "separation of church and state" that is claimed to be required by the United States Constitution.

Thus, this booklet will review a few of the constitutional and other legal issues affecting the religious freedom of churches, with a view to providing churches some information necessary to move forward with their work and ministries.[14]

However, without a true Christianity, churches and their leaders and members are irrelevant—at best. No constitution or law can cure that problem.

Constitutional Foundations

The Religion Clauses in the First Amendment to the United States Constitution's Bill of Rights provide that "Congress shall make no law respecting an establishment of religion, or prohibiting the free exercise thereof . . ."[15] The fact that religion is mentioned first in the First Amendment seems to indicate that, to the Framers, freedom of religion was even more important than freedom of speech and freedom of the press—perhaps even preferred over other rights.

Thus, the First Amendment was designed "to exclude from the national government all power to act on the subject . . . of religion."[16] The Amendment was intended to achieve two goals: first, to prevent the establishment of a national religion; and second, to provide for the accommodation of the rights of religious practice and conscience to promote religious tolerance.[17] A distinct body of law has developed around each of the Religion Clauses, yet each clause has the common purpose "to promote and assure the fullest possible scope of religious liberty and tolerance for all and to nurture the conditions which secure the best hope of attainment of that end."[18]

The religious freedom enshrined in the First Amendment does more than protect individuals. It also protects groups of believers, including organized bodies of individuals known as "churches." In the 1871 case, *Watson v. Jones*,[19] the United States Supreme Court first noted that "[t]he right to organize voluntary religious associations to assist in the expression and dissemination of any religious doctrine . . . is unquestioned."

Thus, the Religion Clauses are the foundation upon which Americans have maintained their individual—and collective—rights to worship and participate in a church organization free from government oppression or direction. Traditionally, these clauses have guaranteed the liberty of churches to act autonomously, operate their organizations, lead their congregations, and speak out on issues of the day free from government interference. James Madison summarized this guarantee, saying, "There is not a shadow of right in the general [federal] government to intermeddle with religion. . . . This subject is, for the honor of America, perfectly free and unshackled. The government has no jurisdiction over it."[20]

The manner in which churches are formed reveals the need for church autonomy. A church is typically formed by a group of two or more believers embracing a common doctrine or belief system. Second, churches have traditionally carried on their activities within the framework of their own ideologies and belief systems without question from the government and secular society.[21]

Professor Douglas Laycock, at the University of Texas, has identified three basic areas of "church rights."[22] First, churches have the fundamental freedom to carry on religious activities—the exercise of religion in its most obvious form. This includes building churches and schools, conducting worship services and praying, and proselytizing and teaching moral values.

The second area involves the right to engage in essential communal activities without outside interference, which includes selecting the church's own leaders, defining the church's own doctrines, resolving the church's own disputes, and running the church's organization.

The third area of church rights is perhaps the most nettlesome. It involves the right of conscientious objection to governmental policy regarding such matters as war, taxes, compulsory education, medical treatment (including inoculations), social insurance, Sabbath observance and nonobservance, monogamy, and other areas that may conflict with the moral precepts of a denomination.

18

Today, however, the right to organize and express religious beliefs, which the Supreme Court and American society once considered unquestionable, is now being scrutinized and the overall deference once shown to religious practice is disappearing.[23]

Traditionally, courts have focused on preventing the establishment of a government religion to ensure the free exercise of religious beliefs. Today, the focus has changed to ensuring toleration for all views at the expense of free exercise. Persons practicing orthodox or traditional religions, Christians in particular, are often not included under the toleration agenda because their beliefs are viewed as too "limiting" and "judgmental" of others.[24] Thus, there is increasing social, cultural and legal pressure for religion to be exercised only in private. For example, in the 1992 graduation prayer case, *Lee v. Weisman*,[25] the Supreme Court decided that "psychological coercion" by the public schools at commencement activities was sufficient to result in an Establishment Clause violation. A vigorously dissenting Justice Antonin Scalia chastised the Justices who comprised the majority, saying: "Church and state would not be such a difficult subject if religion were, as the Court apparently thinks it to be, some purely personal avocation that can be indulged entirely in secret, like pornography, in the privacy of one's room."[26]

Common Legal Concerns

The following are a few of the most common legal concerns of churches.

1 Charitable Immunity

As a general matter, the broad immunity from tort actions (*i.e.*, non-contract or criminal matters) that churches once enjoyed under the doctrine of charitable immunity has largely either been abolished or severely limited, with only a handful of states retaining the concept.

However, where tort liability begins to regulate religious practices, most courts have acknowledged that (1) compelling governmental interests must favor the imposition of liability, (2) such liability must be applied as narrowly as possible to achieve the governmental interest while minimizing the burden on the free exercise of religion, and (3) ample alternative means of religious expression must remain available.

Many cases emphasize a dichotomy between religious *belief* and religious *conduct*, and proceed to minimize the extent to which the Free Exercise Clause protects the latter.

2 Ecclesiastical Abstention Doctrine

This doctrine keeps the courts from taking civil jurisdiction over matters where the courts would have to interpret, evaluate, or resolve religious doctrine or interfere with matters that are integral to the tenets, practices, and administration of an ecclesiastical body. The doctrine is grounded in several Supreme Court cases which have held that decisions of ecclesiastical authorities over matters purely of ecclesiastical significance may generally not be subjected to the judicial review of secular courts unless there is fraud, collusion, or arbitrariness as defined by the church's own policies and procedures.

It must be noted that this doctrine will likely not be applied to matters of liability for negligence which causes injury or damage on church premises, custodial liability, and church day care liabilities.

Church Discipline

Courts generally refuse to recognize actions against churches for expelling a member from fellowship, holding that such conduct is a harm for which the courts recognize no remedy. To recognize such actions as justiciable would raise the risk of unconstitutional state intrusion into ecclesiastical practice that may be fundamentally related to religious beliefs and doctrine.

Where expulsion implicates property and contractual rights, however, courts may reserve the right to resolve such disputes by applying neutral principles of law. For example, in *Randolph v. First Baptist Church,*[27] the court found that the property and contract rights of a church member were violated when the church adopted a new constitution so that it could proceed minutes later to expel the plaintiff. Some courts have held that they may examine the church's constitution, by-laws, and established practices to determine whether or not such discipline has been executed by the correct ecclesiastical authority or body.[28]

Some church members have sought injunctions to prevent their churches from carrying out threats of excommunication, but the majority of courts have denied relief.[29]

4. Expulsion of Contentious Members

Generally speaking, courts will not decide matters involving the expulsion of contentious members under the ecclesiastical abstention doctrine discussed above.[30]

5. Invasion of Privacy

The Free Exercise Clause provides only a limited shield for disciplinary remarks, epithets, and denunciations voiced from the pulpit or other ecclesiastical bodies. Some courts refuse to recognize claims against churches related to invasion of privacy and intentional infliction of emotional distress for disclosing the private sexual affairs of parishioners before a church congregation, holding that the challenged conduct is an ecclesiastical matter of church discipline outside the cognizance of the courts.[31]

The trend, however, seems to be to limit First Amendment protection to discipline directed against voluntary members of the religious community. A church's immunity from tort liability for exposing what it considers the sins of a member ends once it has excommunicated the member or once the individual has chosen to terminate his membership in the church. This distinction is likely grounded in the fiction of implied contract: A member is considered to have contractually consented to church discipline, thereby waiving the church's liability for such discipline. A member who commits a sin under the church doctrine may end the contractual relationship by renouncing his or her association with the church.[32] If the church thereafter publicizes the sin, the member is much more likely to prevail should litigation be initiated.[33]

Some cases have recognized church liability for invasion of privacy where church officials breached assurances of confidentiality made to members caught in affairs.[34]

Indoctrination

This area of concern is especially controversial, and the legal considerations vary, depending on the denomination and particular conduct involved. Thus, issues such as "brainwashing"; seduction; psychological, social, and emotional manipulation; false imprisonment; estrangement; alienation of members from family relationships; and undue influence are beyond the scope of this booklet. For more information on the legal aspects of these issues, contact The Rutherford Institute at the address printed on the copyright page of this booklet.

Medical Care

Criminal liability may be imposed upon parents who neglect to provide medical treatment for their children, even if such treatment violates the religious beliefs of the parents.[35] *However,* few courts have addressed the issue of whether or not civil liability may be imposed upon the *churches* that vigorously discourage medical treatment and impose sanctions upon members who violate such religious tenets.

In *Baumgartner v. First Church of Christ, Scientist,*[36] the court held that allegations of Christian Science malpractice, negligence, and intentional or reckless disregard for health leading to the death of the plaintiff's husband required an inquiry into the tenets of the

Christian Science belief and, thus, such claims were precluded by the First Amendment.

Sex Offenses

Churches have been held liable for sexual offenses by clergy members against minors and members of their congregation.[37] However, matters of child molestation, consensual sex with adult church members, and clergy "malpractice" in sexual conduct are outside the scope of this booklet.

Church Incorporation Issues

A common question posed by pastors and religious leaders concerns whether their churches or religious organizations should incorporate under applicable state laws. The decision whether to incorporate is often not one that is made on purely legal grounds and may involve considerations about the very nature of the church and its work. For some pastors, the idea of forming a corporation to handle church business affairs is tantamount to giving the reigns of the church to the government.[38] Others operate their ministries under the guidelines of their state's nonprofit corporation statute with few reservations. Still others find themselves somewhere in the middle.

Every state and the federal government has a scheme for categorizing groups of persons who coordinate their efforts and handle finances. In this regard, governmental entities do not usually distinguish between the uniquely religious nature of churches from other nonprofit entities. Regardless of how they view themselves, churches are classed by the government with nonprofit organizations in general and must comply with most of the same requirements as other groups to obtain and maintain tax-exempt status. Employment tax reporting, zoning, building and fire codes, and numerous other legal obligations are generally unaffected by corporate status.

A common difficulty incorporated churches have encountered with courts and government agencies is corporate mismanagement. When a church incorporates, it, through its articles of incorporation, is entering into a binding commitment with the state, as well as with the church members, to carry out its business in accordance with established rules for corporate governance, and it must abide by this commitment.

Apart from statutory requirements, nonprofit corporations may construct articles and bylaws as they wish, and they may exercise rather broad discretion in establishing the governing positions and allocations of power within the organization, so long as the general tripartite corporate form of a board of directors, officers, and members is maintained. Churches which incorporate should ensure that their initial corporate documents explicitly reflect the religious nature of the organization. In particular, any doctrinally motivated organizational or operational practices should be plainly stated to have been adopted on that basis.[39]

Where a church is incorporated, compliance with corporate law that is not considered violative of the First Amendment will generally be upheld by the courts.

Another concern confronting churches considering incorporation is liability. There is primarily one notable difference in the legal position of corporations and unincorporated associations: Corporations have a legal "life" of their own. Churches that are not incorporated are generally treated by state and federal courts as unincorporated associations.[40]

A corporation, whether profit or nonprofit, is considered by the law to be a different and separate legal entity than the people who are its members.[41] An unincorporated association, on the other hand, has no legal existence distinct from its members. The legal ramifications include (1) joint and several liability of the individual members themselves for the obligations of the unincorporated association; (2) prohibition of the right of the individual members to sue the unincorporated association for the wrongful act of another member because they are considered

27

coprincipals; and (3) the unincorporated association usually cannot sue or hold property in its own right but must act through designated persons usually called "trustees."

If an unincorporated association is successfully sued and damages are awarded, the plaintiff may collect the award from the personal assets of the members, should the organization lack sufficient insurance coverage or sufficient assets to cover the amount of the judgment.[42]

Furthermore, the liability is considered to be joint and several. This means that the plaintiff could recover damages from any particular member or from all the members.

Another problem with unincorporated churches is the circumstance where a member is injured while working or participating in some church activity. Courts have generally held that the member is incapable of holding the association liable because either they were co-owners of the property on which the mishap occurred, or they were engaged in a joint enterprise and the negligence of one is imputed to all. This stems from the fact that they are agents of each other. This leaves the injured member without a remedy for what might be substantial expenses. Churches that are unincorporated, by virtue of spiritual conviction or otherwise, should make certain that their members are adequately informed of the potential consequences of that election.

The church should thus take steps to alleviate these negative effects of the unincorporated association form. For example, the church could maintain a fund to compensate members injured on church property and maintain adequate insurance coverage for all church activities to cover potential liabilities to third parties, thereby protecting the personal assets of the individuals and families of the church.

Fair Labor Standards Act

The Fair Labor Standards Act ("FLSA") is a federal statute that regulates workplace standards for minimum wages, overtime pay, child labor practices, etc.[43]

Although it is not expressly dealt with by the statute, the FLSA probably does not apply to employees of a church. On the other hand, in *Donovan v. Tony and Susan Alamo Foundation*,[44] the Supreme Court held that the application of wage and hour requirements to a nonprofit religious organization's commercial businesses did not violate the Free Exercise Clause.[45] Application of the requirements did not affect the organization's freedom to worship and evangelize; it merely decreased the available revenue. The commercial activities subject to the act were service stations, retail clothing and grocery outlets, roofing and electrical construction companies, a record-keeping company, a motel, and companies engaged in the production and distribution of candy.[46]

(The minimum wage, maximum hour, and equal-pay-for-equal-job provisions of the FLSA[47] have been found applicable to ministerial employees of church-affiliated schools.)[48]

Immigration Reform and Control Act

Application of the Immigration Reform and Control Act[49] has not been held to violate the free exercise rights of religious organizations whose members' beliefs compelled them to provide employment to persons in need, without regard to residence, nationality, or immigrant status.[50]

However, a federal court of appeals has held that investigative practices by agents of the federal Immigration and Naturalization Service violated the First Amendment rights of churches suspected of participating in the "sanctuary movement" (church-related organizations that provide refuge for immigrants) when the officers entered churches wearing "body bugs" and surreptitiously recorded church services without warrants as part of an undercover investigation.[51]

Employment Issues

In general, the right of church autonomy, stemming from the Free Exercise Clause, has extended "to all aspects of church operations. There is nothing in the cases to indicate that the Supreme Court would disagree. The Court has consistently extended the right of church autonomy as far as necessary to include the cases before it."[52]

Specifically, church labor relations fall within the purview of church autonomy. Deciding how the church's work will be conducted is an essential part of the exercise of religion. According to the Supreme Court, labor relations are matters of church administration; undoubtedly, they affect the operation of churches.[53]

Federal statutes provide that certain employers are not allowed to discriminate among their employees or applicants on the basis of race, color, religion, sex, or national origin.[54] Title VII of the Civil Rights Act of 1964, the primary statute in the area of employment discrimination, provides that it does not apply to:

> [R]eligious corporation, association, educational institution, or society with respect to the employment of individuals of a particular religion to perform work connected with the carrying on by such corporation, association, educational institution, or society of its activities.[55]

Thus, the church generally may not discriminate based on race, color, sex, or national origin, but it may discriminate based on religion in order to employ only those who agree with their religious beliefs.[56]

With the growing number of laws protecting sexual orientation from discrimination, there is a concern that such laws may force churches to operate contrary to their religious beliefs. A number of states have already enacted anti–sexual orientation discrimination legislation. Despite much debate to the contrary, a new right is being created since the status of sexual orientation has not yet been found to be protected under the Fourteenth Amendment's Equal Protection Clause as a suspect, or even a quasi-suspect classification.[57]

Although federal standards are the basis for many civil rights laws, other governmental bodies may choose to create additional legislation in order to heighten protection against discrimination. At various levels of federal, state, and local government, sexual orientation is sometimes protected under general human rights provisions. The effect of such laws on churches has significant potential.

Thus, in *The Presbytery of New Jersey of the Orthodox Presbyterian Church v. Florio*,[58] a case handled by The Rutherford Institute, the plaintiffs asserted that amendments to New Jersey's Law Against Discrimination[59] ("LAD") violated their First Amendment right to freedom of speech.[60] Specifically, LAD prohibits discrimination on the basis of sexual orientation in employment; labor organization membership; public accommodations; and real estate, financial, and business transactions.[61] However, LAD is a carefully constructed statute in that it exempts religious organizations from compliance in the selection of their own employees, and it permits religious organizations to restrict rental or use of their own property to members of their own faith.[62]

Relying on a state official's affidavit that the state would not enforce LAD against the plaintiff churches or the plaintiff pastor, a trial court held that the case was not ripe for decision by the court. After a remand by a federal appeals court, the trial court concluded that the statute precluded the right of the pastor, as an individual, to disseminate anything expressing opposition to homosexual acts.[63] The case is under appeal as of this writing.

The outcome of this case may have an impact on similarly proposed or existing state legislation. Despite LAD's "religious exemption," religious persons will still be affected because, as the federal appeals court noted, it is not sufficient to conclude that an individual is unaffected by LAD simply because he or she would not be prosecuted in his or her institutional capacity (i.e., as a minister) under LAD.[64] In short, LAD's restrictiveness on religious persons in a nonprofessional or nonministerial context is still at issue. To the extent that pastors do not believe they operate or live in a "nonministerial context," this is a significant issue.[65]

Americans with Disabilities Act

The Act provides that no individual shall be discriminated against on the basis of disability in the full and equal enjoyment of the goods, services, facilities, privileges, advantages, or accommodations of any place of public accommodation by any person who owns, leases (or leases to), or operates a place of public accommodation.[66] However, the Act expressly exempts religious organizations, or entities controlled by religious organizations, from its provisions.[67] Thus, a church is not required by the law to make its sanctuary accessible, for example, to individuals with disabilities, nor would new church facilities be required to be constructed to be accessible.[68] If a church operates a school or a day care center, it would not be subject to the requirements of the Act.[69] The test is whether the church or other religious organization operates the public accommodation, not which individuals receive the public accommodation's services.[70] Notwithstanding the law, however, it would seem that churches would make every effort to include those with disabilities in their activities.

Despite the exemption from facilities requirements, religious organizations are still subject to the prohibitions on hiring discrimination against persons with disabilities. However, religious organizations may still give preference to individuals of a particular religion to perform its work and to require that all applicants and employees conform to the religious tenets of the organization.[71]

Access to Public Facilities

The Supreme Court held in the 1993 case *Lamb's Chapel v. Center Moriches Union Free School District*[72] that a school district violated the Establishment Clause when it refused to allow a church to use school property to show a six-part film series on instilling family values. The film would have been permitted by school policy were it not for its religious theme.

The Court ruled that "there would have been no realistic danger that the community would think that the District was endorsing religion or any particular creed, and any benefit to religion or to the Church would have been no more than incidental."[73]

The Supreme Court also held that the church's freedom of speech, guaranteed through the First and Fourteenth Amendments, was violated by the denial of access to school property. After permitting other groups to use its property for social or civic purposes, the school denied the church the same right based on the film's religious perspective. Such a basis for the denial was invalid under the Court's holding in *Cornelius v. NAACP Legal Defense and Educational Fund, Inc.*[74] that access to speakers in nonpublic forums may not be denied solely to suppress a particular point of view on a topic encompassed within the forum.

"Landmarking" Church Property

An issue regarding church control of property involves works of art located within a church or architectural features of "historical" interest that become protected as "landmarks" or similar designations. Problems arise when laws or ordinances attempt to protect such works and churches seek to remove or change them. Court decisions have gone both ways on this subject. For assistance on such matters, contact The Rutherford Institute at the address listed on the copyright page of this booklet.[75]

Zoning Issues

Zoning issues and church rights collide primarily when zoning laws conflict with the desire of a church to establish or alter a church in a designated geographic area.

If a city, county, zoning board, or other municipal authority determines that a building or place of assembly does not qualify under the applicable definition of "church," then that authority may try to deny the church permission to operate in districts or zones where churches otherwise are permitted.

But courts have historically recognized the expansiveness of the terms "church" and "religion." A New York court of appeals stated:

> A church is more than merely an edifice affording people the opportunity to worship God. Strictly religious uses and activities are more than prayer and sacrifice and all churches recognize that the area of their responsibility is broader than leading the congregation in prayer. . . . To limit a church to being merely a house of prayer and sacrifice would, in a large degree, be depriving the church of the opportunity of enlarging, perpetuating and strengthening itself and the congregation.[76]

Courts have thus recognized many church activities as religious and customary church functions for zoning purposes.[77]

On the other hand, other courts have refused to provide for zoning allowances for church day care centers,[78] a pastoral counseling center,[79] a homeless shelter[80] or otherwise tried to prevent organized worship in certain locales.

A case in point is *Geisinsky v. Village of Kings Point*,[81] which was handled by The Rutherford Institute. In this case, the defendant-village threatened enforcement of a zoning code to prohibit a Lubavitch rabbi from erecting a canopy adjacent to his residence to protect worshippers from inclement weather at an outdoor celebration of Yom Kippur and Rosh Hashanah. The village subsequently moved to prohibit the rabbi from meeting with other congregants for weekly prayer and worship. The village contended that use of the premises in this fashion converted a single-family residence to a "house of worship," thereby subjecting the activity to a host of regulations applicable to church buildings. The court ruled that by enforcing zoning regulations in this manner, the village had violated the plaintiffs' rights protected under the Religious Freedom Restoration Act of 1993 ("RFRA")[82] and also the New York public policy that requires that every effort be made to accommodate religious uses of property.

In *Western Presbyterian Church v. Board of Zoning of the District of Columbia*,[83] the court also held that the city zoning board's decision to prohibit the church from resuming its program for feeding the poor at a new location violated RFRA.[84] The court reasoned that the zoning board's decision substantially burdened the church's exercise of an integral facet of its religious beliefs, namely, the feeding of the poor at its facility.[85] Meanwhile, the court concluded that the zoning board could show no compelling interest in prohibiting the church program, in that, to date, there was no evidence that it was a nuisance to the community.[86]

In *United States v. Village of Airmont*,[87] a case handled by The Rutherford Institute, the court ruled on an action for injunctive relief by the United States Government, alleging that a village zoning ordinance was in violation of the Fair Housing Act.[88] The government specifically alleged that the ordinance could potentially limit the ability of Hasidic Jews in the village from holding home worship services.[89] The trial court noted that if zoning laws make the exercise of religion inaccessible to practitioners, the laws may amount to a violation of First Amendment rights.[90]

The court of appeals reversed a majority of the trial court's finding, stating that:

> The events cited . . . as evincing a need for Airmont's incorporation and gaining control of zoning amply supported a finding that the impetus was not a legitimate nondiscriminatory reason but rather an animosity toward Orthodox Jews as a group.[91]

This decision is currently on appeal.

Some courts have provided churches with immunity from zoning laws. The reasoning in *Church of Jesus Christ of Latter-Day Saints v. Jefferson County*,[92] exemplifies this approach. In this case, a federal court stated:

When . . . a community's zoning plan infringes upon first amendment rights, we scrutinize its validity more closely, and mere rationality of the plan does not suffice: it must be narrowly drawn in furtherance of a substantial government interest. We use this more stringent standard even when a challenged regulation restricts freedom of expression only incidentally or only in a small number of cases.[93]

The government does not have the authority to determine what is a legitimate ministry of a church because such a determination violates both the Establishment and the Free Exercise Clauses of the First Amendment.[94] Thus, activities of a church that are mandated as part of the church's religious tenets should be permitted under the Religion Clauses of the First Amendment.

Political Action and Tax-exempt Status

Internal Revenue Service Publication 1828 entitled "Tax Guide for Churches and Other Religious Organizations" discusses the § 501(c)(3) tax exemptions and the accompanying restrictions.

Generally, a § 501(c)(3) tax-exempt organization is prevented from "attempting to influence legislation" and intervene politically. An organization is designated as "attempting to influence legislation" if an organization's legislative activity constitutes a "substantial part" of its overall activities.

On the other hand, whether an action constitutes political intervention is not measured by a "substantial part" standard.

The IRS notes that all § 501(c)(3) organizations, including churches, are prohibited from participating in, or intervening in (including the publication or distribution of statements), any political campaign on behalf of (or in opposition to) any candidate for public office. The IRS states that violation of this prohibition results in denial or revocation of exempt status and the imposition of certain excise taxes.

Again, the IRS says that:

> . . . [C]ertain voter education activities (including the presentation of public forums and the publication of voter education guides) conducted in a nonpartisan manner may not constitute prohibited political activity, while other so-called voter education activities may. Contributions to political campaign funds, public statements of position (verbal and written) in favor of or in opposition to candidates for office, or provision of a forum for expression of candidates' views on a partisan basis, however, would clearly violate the prohibition against political activity.

The political activity prohibition is not intended to restrict free expression on political matters by leaders of religious organizations speaking for themselves as individuals. Ministers and others who commonly speak or write on behalf of religious organizations should clearly indicate, at the time they do so, that public comments made by them in connection with political campaigns are strictly personal and are not intended to represent their organization. Partisan comments by the employees or other representatives of an organization regarding political candidates must be avoided in official organization publications and at official church functions.

Besides losing its tax exemption under § 501(c)(3) for engaging in political activities, an organization is also subject to an excise tax on its political expenditures and is required to correct the violation.

Although the IRS attempts to make the area of church tax exemption appear clear-cut, this has not been the outcome in the courts. Rather, the courts have struggled with this issue and have had varying results. Nowhere is this disparity more apparent than in the decisions of the United States Supreme Court.[95] However, despite the Supreme Court's inconsistent analysis of tax exemptions for churches and other religious organizations under the Establishment Clause, four basic conclusions may be made concerning such Establishment Clause analysis.

First, tax exemptions for religious institutions are a privilege and not a constitutional right.

Second, members of the Court disagree on the classification or characterization of the tax exemption. Some Justices apparently do not view tax exemptions as subsidies[96] while other Justices equate these concepts.[97]

Third, the Court invariably considers whether the tax exemption benefits only religious groups or a more general class of interests.[98]

Finally, tax exemptions heretofore protected under the Establishment Clause are subordinated to "matters of national public policy" or to other rights.[99]

With the pro-IRS sentiment demonstrated by the courts and the anti-church stance taken by much of modern government, it is perhaps time that churches take a different approach to tax-exemption of religious activity. At a time when much of the Judeo-Christian moral structure is decaying in America and the church appears to be less and less involved and relevant to modern society, the time may be near when the church should override concerns about the deductibility of donations and the exclusion of the church's income from taxation in order to enter vigorously the political marketplace.

Jesus Christ exhorted Christians, and, of course the church, to be "the salt of the earth" and "the light of the world."[100]

At this point in history, where politicians are making decisions concerning abortion, education, and other central matters, there may be no greater time than now for the church to act and influence, not only the political, but all facets of society. This may require forgetting such things as fighting for tax-exempt status, which consumes valuable time and resources, and concentrating on the crucial civic and legal battlefields, areas that are eroding as we speak. It is only by putting full effort into those areas, such as the political realm, that the church can truly answer Christ's call and become "the salt of the earth" and "the light of the world."

The Future

The Constitution was written by people who were well aware of the opposition to religious liberty throughout history and by some of their contemporaries. They also knew that even the truly religious may inevitably be corrupted and attempt to use religion to gain power or wealth. As a result, the Framers of our government attempted to create a system where religious liberty for everyone could thrive.[101] As I have written elsewhere:

> As secularism imposes its worldview on society, we can only expect continuing and increasing interference with the rights, liberties, and even the lives of humankind. The result will be an on-

going conflict between traditional theism and pervasive secular ideologies.[102]

But if all churches regain their focus and their true Christianity, secularists and the government will be compelled to return at least to a "positive neutrality" and the accommodation of religious liberty required by the Constitution.

Notes

1. Mark A. Noll, Nathan O. Hatch, George M. Marsden, David F. Wells, and John D. Woodbridge, eds., *Eerdmans' Handbook to Christianity in America* (Grand Rapids: Eerdmans, 1983), 144.

2. *Ibid.*

3. Albert Marrin, *The War for Independence: The Story of the American Revolution* (New York: Atheneum, 1988), 45.

4. Patricia U. Banomi, *Under the Cape of Heaven: Religion, Society and Politics in Colonial America* (New York: Oxford Univ. Press, 1986), 211.

5. *See* John W. Whitehead, *Religious Apartheid: The Separation of Religion from American Public Life* (Chicago: Moody, 1994), especially 163–94.

6. Richard N. Ostling, "The Church Search," *Time*, 5 April 1993, 47; in Whitehead, *Religious Apartheid*, 147.

7. Mark Twain, quoted by Justin Kaplan, "How God Made It Only Religiously Neutral American Money," *Los Angeles Daily Journal*, 9 October 1992; in Whitehead, *Religious Apartheid*, 146.

8. George Gallup, Jr., and William Proctor, *Forecast 2000: George Gallup, Jr. Predicts the Future of America* (New York: William

Morrow, 1984), 153; in Whitehead, *Religious Apartheid*, 164–65.

9. John R. Stott, *Christ the Controversialist* (Downers Grove, Ill.: InterVarsity, 1970), 182; in Whitehead, *Religious Apartheid*, 166.

10. Mark 13:32.

11. Neil Postman, *Amusing Ourselves to Death: Public Discourse in the Age of Show Business* (New York: Viking, 1985), 116–17; in Whitehead, *Religious Apartheid*, 171–72.

12. Postman, *Amusing Ourselves to Death*, 55–56; in Whitehead, *Religious Apartheid*, 175.

13. 1 Peter 4:17.

14. The comments and information in this booklet are intended to provide a framework for action and are not intended to provide specific legal advice. As in any legal situation, specific facts may affect the application or interpretation of the law. Thus, one should always seek competent legal advice for a particular situation prior to making any decision on a legal matter.

15. U.S. Const. amend. 1.

16. Edward S. Corwin, *American Constitutional History* (New York: Harper Torchbooks, 1965), 205.

17. *See* Daniel Dreisbach, *Real Threat and Mere Shadow* (Westchester, Ill.: Crossway, 1987), 83–96.

18. *Wallace v. Jaffree*, 472 U.S. 38 (O'Connor, J., concurring); *School Dist. of Abington Twsp. v. Schempp*, 374 U.S. 203, 305 (1963) (Goldberg, J., concurring).

19. 80 U.S. 679, 728, 729 (1871).

20. James Madison, *The Writings of James Madison*, ed. Gaillard Hunt (New York: Putnam, 1900–1910), 5:132, 176.

21. Gerard V. Bradley, *Church Autonomy in the Constitutional Order: The End of Church and State?*, 49 LA. L. REV. 1057 (1989).

22. Douglas Laycock, *Towards a General Theory of the Religion Clauses: The Case of Church Labor Relations and the Right to Church Autonomy*, 81 COLUM. L. REV. 1373, 1388–90 (1981).

23. *See, e.g., Lee v. Weisman*, 112 S. Ct. 2649 (1992).

24. Whitehead, *Religious Apartheid*, 154.

25. 112 S. Ct. 2649 (1992).

26. *Id.* at 2685 (Scalia, J., dissenting).

27. 120 N.E.2d 485 (Ohio Com. Pl. 1954).

28. *See Baugh v. Thomas*, 265 A.2d 675, 677 (N.J. 1970) (civil courts have jurisdiction to determine whether the church's constitution, bylaws, and other conventional procedures have been followed in expelling a member of the congregation); *First Baptist Church of Glen Este v. State of Ohio*, 591 F. Supp. 676, 683 (S.D. Ohio 1983). But see *Fowler v. Bailey*, 844 P.2d 141, 144 (Okl. 1992) (holding that membership in a religious community is not a legally valuable right, so there is no remedy if one is excommunicated by unconventional means).

29. *See, e.g., Alexander v. Shiloh Baptist Church*, 592 N.E.2d 918 (Ohio Com. Pl. 1991) (refusing to grant preliminary injunction against the church to prevent it from carrying out threats of excommunication against members who were pursuing litigation against it, since it would violate the free exercise rights of the church); *Davis v. Church of Jesus Christ*, 852 P.2d 640 (Mont. 1993) (holding that evidence of religious sanctions, including denial of Temple Recommend, denial of church calling, and threats of excommunication were not admissible evidence in actions against the church, which at-

tempted to discourage plaintiff from pursuing her claims to recover for injuries sustained on church premises).

But see Kennedy v. Gray, 807 P.2d 670 (Kan. 1991) (holding that members who were expelled after bringing a suit for accounting of Pleasant Green Baptist Church's financial affairs were entitled to due process in explusion proceedings).

30. *See, e.g., O'Connor v. Diocese of Honolulu*, 885 P.2d 361 (Hawaii 1994). *See also Burgess v. Rock Creek Baptist Church*, 734 F. Supp. 30 (D.D.C. 1990 (doctrine of ecclesiastical abstention precluded court from recognizing action against church and church leaders for intentional infliction of emotional distress arising out of church's termination and transfer of her membership to another church). *But see First Baptist Church of Glen Este v. State of Ohio*, 591 F. Supp. 676 (S.D.Ohio 1983).

31. *See Rasmussen v. Bennett*, 741 P.2d 755 (Mont. 1987) (denouncements made within Jehovah's Witnesses congregation accusing couple of "conduct unbecoming Christians" and referring to them as "filth" were based on religious doctrine, so their veracity was not determinable by the court); *Korean Presbyterian Church v. Lee*, 880 P.2d 565 (Wash. App. 1994) (holding that ecclesiastical abstention doctrine precluded five ex-members from recovery for alleged outrageous conduct by church officials for announcing their excommunications from the pulpit).

32. *See Hadnot v. Shaw*, 826 P.2d 978, 989 (Okl. 1992) ("At the point when the church-member relationship is severed through an *affirmative act either of* a parishioner's withdrawal *or of excommunication* by the ecclesiastical body. . . . the absolute privilege from tort liability no longer attaches") (emphasis in the original); *Hester v. Barnett*, 723 S.W.2d 544 (Mo. App. 1987) (no First Amendment

privilege for Baptist minister who violated confidential counseling relationship with nonmember couple and falsely accused them of child abuse, fraud, theft, and arson; denouncing them from the pulpit, church publications, and in neighborhood meetings he organized and directed).

33. *See Guinn v. Church of Christ*, 775 P.2d 766 (Okl. 1989).

34. *See St. Luke Evangelical Lutheran Church, Inc. v. Smith*, 568 A.2d 35 (Md. 1990) (upholding a $337,000 verdict, including punitive damages, in an action for defamation and invasion of privacy against church and associate pastor who intruded into church employee's office, searched her files, and found letters from another associate pastor intimating an affair between them, and disclosing this information to relatives of the two paramours and to various members of the church); *Snyder v. Evangelical Orthodox Church*, 264 Cal. Rptr. 640 (App. 1989) (holding that Superior Court had subject matter jurisdiction over intentional infliction of emotional distress and related claims against church made by bishop and his paramour whose confession of a sexual affair was publicly exposed before the congregation though the bishops to whom they confessed had promised to keep their confession in confidence). *See also Alberts v. Devine*, 479 N.E.2d 113 (Mass.), *cert. denied*, 474 U.S. 1013 (1985).

35. *See Walker v. Superior Court of California*, 763 P.2d 852 (Cal. 1988), *cert. denied*, 491 U.S. 905 (1989) (holding that parents who utilized prayer in lieu of medical treatment for their four-year-old daughter, who endured seventeen days of meningitis and then died, could be prosecuted for involuntary manslaughter and felony child-endangerment, despite the presence of exemptions in child neglect and welfare statutes for parents who substi-

tute medical care with prayer). In many states, there are statutory exemptions from child neglect and abuse laws for religious parents who substitute prayer for regular medical care. When parents have been acquitted of criminal liability, it has often been on grounds of statutory vagueness. Several courts have held that the applicable state child protection statutes fail to fairly notify parents when their conduct loses statutory protection and becomes subject to criminal liability, thus depriving them of due process of law. *See Brown v. Laitner*, 435 N.W.2d 1 (Mich. 1989); *State v. McKown*, 475 N.W.2d 63 (Minn. 1991), *cert. denied*, 112 S. Ct. 882 (1992); *Hermanson v. State*, 604 So.2d 775 (Fla. 1992); *Commonwealth v. Twitchell*, 617 N.E.2d 609 (Mass. 1993). But none of these cases predicated acquittal on free exercise grounds.

36. 490 N.E.2d 1319 (Ill. App. Div. 1986), *cert. denied*, 479 U.S. 915 (1986).

37. *See* 5 ALR 5th at 535–36.

38. This fear is not entirely unfounded. Several courts have held that where a church avails itself of a state's nonprofit corporation statutes, it has submitted itself to the jurisdiction of state courts in matters of a "corporate nature." *Matthews v. Adams*, 520 So. 2d 334 (Fla. App. 1988), *Thomas v. Craig*, 424 So. 2d 1090 (La. App. 1982).

39. *See, e.g., Gipson v. Brown*, 288 Ark. 422, 706 S.W.2d 369 (1986).

40. R. Hammer, *Pastor, Church and Law* (Christian Ministry Resources, 1991), 269.

41. Phillip I. Blumberg, *The Law of Corporate Groups* (New York: Little Brown, 1987).

42. *Ibid.*

43. 29 U.S.C. §§ 201–19 (1978, Supp. 1991).

44. 471 U.S. 290 (1985).

45. *Id.* at 290.

46. *Id.* at 291–92.

47. 29 U.S.C. §§ 206(a) and (d) (1988).

48. *See DeArment v. Harvey*, 932 F.2d 721 (8th Cir. 1991); *Dole v. Shenandoah Baptist Church*, 899 F.2d 1389 (4th Cir.), *cert. denied*, 111 S.Ct. 131 (1990).

49. 8 U.S.C. § 1324(a) (1986).

50. *See Intercommunity Center for Justice and Peace v. I.N.S.*, 910 F.2d 42 (2d Cir. 1990) (Catholic community center not exempt); *American Friends Serv. Comm. v. Thornberg*, 718 F. Supp. 820 (C.D. Cal. 1989), *aff'd*, 941 F.2d 808 (2d Cir. 1990) (Quaker organization not exempt); *American Baptist Churches v. Meese*, 666 F. Supp. 1358 (N.D. Cal. 1987) (First Amendment rights of sanctuary workers not violated).

51. *Presbyterian Church v. United States*, 870 F.2d 518 (9th Cir. 1989), *on remand*, 752 F. Supp. 1505 (D. Ariz. 1990).

52. Douglas Laycock, *Towards a General Theory of the Religion Clauses: The Case of Church Labor Relations and the Right to Church Autonomy*, 81 COLUM. L. REV. 1373, 1397 (1981).

53. *Serbian Eastern Orthodox Diocese v. Milivojevich*, 426 U.S. 696 (1976); *Jones v. Wolf*, 443 U.S. 595, 605 (1979); *see* Ripple, *The Entanglement Test of the Religion Clauses—A Ten Year Assessment*, 27 U.C.L.A. L. REV. 1195, 1214 (1980) n. 138, citing *Kedroff v. Saint Nicholas Cathedral of the Russian Orthodox Church*, 344 U.S. 94, 107 (1952).

54. 42 U.S.C. Sec. 2000e-17 (1988).

55. 42 U.S.C. Sec. 2000e-1 (1988).

56. *See McClure v. Salvation Army*, 460 F.2d. 553 (5th Cir.) *cert. denied* as untimely filed, 409 U.S. 896 (1972) (sex discrimination allowed); *EEOC v. Southern Baptist Seminary*, 485 F. Supp. 255 (N.D.Tex. 1980), rev'd in part, 651 F.2d 277 (5th Cir.

1981), *cert. denied*, 456 U.S. 905 (1982) (sex discrimination allowed).

57. *National Gay Task Force v. Board of Educ. of City of Oklahoma City*, 729 F.2d 1270, 1273 (10th Cir. 1984), aff'd, 470 U.S. 903 (1985); *High Tech Gays v. Defense Indus. Sec. Clearance Office*, 895 F.2d 563 (9th Cir. 1990).

58. 40 F.3d 1454 (3d Cir. 1994).

59. N.J. Stat. Ann. Secs 10:5-1 to 10:5-42 (West 1993 & Supp. 1994). The statute added to the category of impermissible distinctions "affectional or sexual orientation" to the statute's ban on forms of discrimination.

60. *Florio*, 40 F.3d at 1458.

61. Unpublished opinion of the United States District Court for the District of New Jersey, No. 92-1641 (WGB), *slip. op.* at 65 (September 13, 1995).

62. 40 F.3d at 1459.

63. *Id.* at 1460.

64. *Id.* at 1468.

65. *See, e.g.*, Lincoln C. Oliphant, *What Churches Can Expect from "Gay Rights" Laws: A Preview of Iowa's Sexual Orientation Bill*, 33 Cath. Law. 87, 106 (1990).

66. 42 U.S.C. Sec. 12182.

67. 42 U.S.C. Sec. 12187.

68. Exempt Facilities, Accommodating Disabilities (CCH) Sec. 10, 150 (1994).

69. *Id.*

70. *Id.*

71. 42 U.S.C. Sec. 12113(c)(1) and (2).

72. 113 S. Ct. 2141 (1993).

73. *Id.* at 2148.

74. 473 U.S. 788 (1985).

75. Sandy Coleman, "Church's Rights Prevail in Art Case," *Boston Globe*, 14 July 1992, 63.

76. *Community Synagogue v. Bates,* 136 N.E.2d 488, 493 (1956).

77. *See St. John's Evangelical Lutheran Church v. Hoboken,* 479 A.2d 935, 937–38 (1983) (providing shelter for the homeless); *Unitarian Universalist Church of Central Nassau v. Shorten,* 314 N.Y.S.2d 66, 70–72 (1970) (a day care center on church facilities); *Slevin v. Long Island Jewish Medical Center,* 319 N.Y.S.2d 937 (1971) (running a drug center for youth located in a parish house).

78. *In re Covenant Community Church, Inc.,* 444 N.Y.S.2d 415 (N.Y. Sup. 1981).

79. *Needham Pastoral Counseling Center v. Board of Appeals of Needham,* 557 N.E.2d 43 (Mass. App. Ct. 1990).

80. *First Assembly of God of Naples v. Collier County,* 20 F.3d 419 (11th Cir. 1994), *cert. denied,* 115 S. Ct. 730, modified, 27 F.3d 526, *cert. denied,* 115 S. Ct. 730 (1994).

81. No. 25625-94 (Sup. Ct. N.Y., Nassau County, 15 December 1994).

82. Discussed *infra.*

83. 862 F. Supp. 538 (D.D.C. 1994).

84. *Id.* at 547.

85. *Id.* at 544.

86. *Id.* In contrast, in *Germantown Seventh-Day Adventist Church v. City of Philadelphia* [_____ F. Supp. _____, 1994 U.S. Dist. LEXIS 12163 (E.D. Pa. 1994), *aff'd per curiam,* No. 94–1889 (3d Cir. 1995)], the court held RFRA inapplicable to a dispute in which the city rejected the church's application for a permit to construct an addition to its existing facilities because the church's plans did not demonstrate a sufficient off-street parking to comply with the zoning requirements (1994 U.S. Dist. LEXIS 12163 at 1). The church revised its plans, obtained permission to proceed, was later forced to stop because of calculation errors, but af-

terward, it was allowed to continue. The court granted summary judgment to the city, simply stating that the church had "utterly failed to show that anyone's freedom of religion was affected, let alone 'substantially burden[ed],' by the City's zoning provisions" under RFRA. *Id.* at 3.

87. 839 F. Supp. 1054 (S.D.N.Y. 1993), 1995 U.S. App. LEXIS 27174.

88. 42 U.S.C. Secs. 3601 *et seq.*

89. 839 F. Supp. at 1066.

90. *Id., citing Islamic Center of Miss. v. Starkville, Miss.,* 840 F.2d 293 (5th Cir. 1988). However, in this case, the court denied injunctive relief because it reasoned that free exercise did not give worshipers a veto over government programs or regulations that do not prohibit the free exercise of religion. *Id.,* citing *Lyng v. Northwest Indian Cemetery Protective Ass'n,* 485 U.S. 439 (1987).

91. 1995 U.S.App. LEXIS 27174 at 53.

92. 741 F. Supp. 1522 (N.D.Ala. 1990).

93. *Id.* at 1531, 1532.

94. *See Thomas v. Review Bd.,* 450 U.S. 707 (1981).

95. *See Walz v. Tax Comm'n,* 397 U.S. 664–75 (1970); *Bob Jones University v. United States,* 461 U.S. 574 (1983); *Texas Monthly, Inc. v. Bullock,* 489 U.S. 1 (1989); *Jimmy Swaggart Ministries v. Board of Equalization,* 493 U.S. 378 (1990).

96. *See, e.g., Regan v. Taxation with Representation,* 461 U.S. 540, 544 n.5 (1983); *Walz v. Tax Comm'n,* 397 U.S. 664, 675–76, 690–91 (1970).

97. *See, e.g., Texas Monthly, Inc. v. Bullock,* 489 U.S. 1, 14–15 (1989).

98. This factor may change, given the dissenting opinion in *Texas Monthly,* in which three Justices deemed this consideration irrelevant. *Texas Monthly,* 489 U.S. at 35–36.

99. *See, e.g., Bob Jones Univ. v. United States,* 461 U.S. 574 (1983) (religion rights inferior to issues concerning public policy); *Texas Monthly,* 489 U.S. at 26–27 (Blackmun, J., concurring) (accusing other Justices of preferring one First Amendment value over another).

100. Matthew 5:13–14.

101. Whitehead, *Religious Apartheid,* 169.

102. *Ibid.,* 209.